The Credo

8 Simple virtues for living with passion and purpose in the post-truth era

CLIFF HARVEY

www.cliffharvey.com

Katoa Health Publishing

ISBN:

978-0-9941313-8-6 (paperback)

978-0-9941313-9-3 (eBook)

CONTENTS

Preface 1

But what's the point? 2

The Virtue in Happiness 4

A new Eudaemonism. Redux 6

Happiness vs Ecstasy 6

My Story 9

But wait! There's more… 24

A note on reflections 25

A note on commitments 25

Honesty 27

Reflection: 29

Commitment: 30

Humility 31

Reflections: 35

Commitment: 35

Respect 37

Reflections: 39

Commitment: 40

Loyalty 41

Reflections:..43

Commitment: 43

Courage 45

Your Values & Ethos 46

The Courage to Change 48

Reflections:..50

Commitment: 51

Part 2. Creativity, Passion, and Purpose 53

Creativity 55

Reflections:..60

Commitment: 60

Purpose 61

Reflections:..63

Commitment: 63

Passion..65

One final note… 67

Part 3. Integration 69

Mindfulness..71

Action: 75

Mindfulness of breath 75

Gratitude... 79

    Action:... 80

Gratitude and Forgiveness.. 81

Beliefs... 85

    Action:... 86

    'Flipping' negative belief patterns 87

Check-ins... 89

    Action:... 93

Breaks... 95

Daily Breaks 95

Self-appointments & Weekly Breaks 96

Periodic Breaks 98

    Action:... 100

After... 103

About Cliff.. 105

PREFACE

What is living with passion and purpose?

Nowadays, I can't help but feel that many of the people I work with as a health practitioner, either directly or indirectly, are confused and lack direction. This leads them to leap from one flight of fancy to another, constantly searching for the next hit, whether it is that next hit of sugar, drugs, alcohol, sexual partner or hit show on the box. Now, I'm not going to sit here and write that any of the above is *wrong* because the moral garbage we wrap around what is and isn't *right* or *wrong* is straight up bullshit. An altogether arbitrary idea of right or wrong has no worthwhile role to play in whether the lives we live are, on balance, happy and fulfilling.

More important than arbitrary morality, is to have a values-driven life. In other words, it's having a clear idea of your moral compass, and more importantly, knowing *why* those values that you hold dear are important to you.

Rest assured I make no claim to be the perfect example of the Credo I outline in this book. I have fucked up on multiple occasions in my life and I will, I'm sure, continue to fuck things up from time to time... But I try to live *with* this Credo as a guiding light for how to act in life, to become a better version of me. It provides something to come back to when I slip-up so I can learn from my mistakes and see them as not as an aberration, but instead as an integral part of the process of life and an opportunity to learn, grow, and evolve.

WHAT STANDS IN THE WAY, BECOMES THE WAY

MARCUS AURELIAS

But what's the point?

Good question, I'm glad I asked...

People think I'm being negative or nihilist when I say frankly "There is no point"…

But I'm not.

People that don't know me well might interpret some of the things I say as morose or moribund, but they aren't negative per se. When I say there's no point, I mean that there really is no singular, encapsulated 'thing' that defines why we are on this freakin' planet, living this human existence. If you know of one, then congrats, you're way ahead of me.

If I had to say anything, I'd say that overall, *the key to life is to be happy*. However, when I say this, I tend to get eye-rolls and palpable looks of "really bro?" only barely concealed on people's faces. It's almost become the *concept du jour* to think of the pursuit of happiness as naïve, simplistic, and ultimately self-defeating. Conversely, people talk a lot about the supposedly superior approach of seeking purpose over happiness, but, in my humble opinion, these are flip sides of the same coin.

Think about it this way; if someone were to ask you what you really want in life, would you be more likely to answer, "I want to be happy" or, "I want to have a purpose"? I can guarantee that most people would say that they want to be happy.

Happiness is a state of being and it's one that people want to exist within. On the other hand, purpose is 'doing'. It is a framework of action that allows us to live in a way that achieves the state of being (happiness) that we desire. So, the two are not opposed, but instead, *happiness* (on balance) is the outcome, and *purpose* is the way to achieve that outcome.

Living with purpose is a way for us to define the actions of a 'good' life. The actions of life are how we influence the world around us, and the direction that we will take within that world. So, if we can agree that our lives and our 'selves' are defined by our actions within a life of purpose, we must then decide, *what defines the 'rightness' of our actions?*

If happiness is the outcome of an objectively desirable life, then it stands to reason that what is most right is that which creates the greatest amount of happiness.

THE VIRTUE IN HAPPINESS

Eudaemonia is often directly translated into English as 'happiness', but this is not entirely accurate. The word derives from the ancient Greek *eu* meaning 'good' or 'in balance' and -*daemon*, 'spirit', and so, the word has a broader meaning of happiness as a state of a good spirit, and a state of *being* that is in balance. *Arete* is the other central concept of Ancient Greek ethics. Arete means broadly 'excellence' but has the particular meaning of 'virtue', especially in relation to knowledge. *Eudaemonism* is the moral theory that links *arete* with *eudaemonia* and therefore, describes 'the virtue of happiness'. Socrates, Plato, Epicurus and, perhaps most importantly, Aristotle and the Stoic philosophers discussed the nuances of eudaemonism. In Aristotle's *Nicomachean Ethics*, eudaemonia is considered the highest aim of human thinking and endeavour and is something that is achieved through action (of the *psyche* or soul). Aristotelian ethics was considered by Aristotle himself to be unique, in that it was practical rather than simply theoretical. The Stoics, also remarkably practical in their philosophy, described eudaemonism in their teachings as the 'good life' – one of action, and one that is morally virtuous.

So, eudaemonism is a concept that can provide a guide for what we do in our lives.

A new Eudaemonism. Redux

I wrote about a 'new eudaemonism' many years ago in one of my very first books. The premise was simple; that 'right action' is that which promotes happiness and therefore what is 'most right' is that which promotes the greatest amount of *net* happiness. I described this as a code of ethics summarised into one simple sentence: *That which is most right is that which creates the greatest net happiness,* and that we can use a logical razor (Harvey's razor!) to evaluate our actions, i.e. *The 'rightness' of an action is determined by how much happiness that action creates.*

Happiness vs Ecstasy

The question arises; if 'right action' is concerned with creating happiness, then does that mean we should be selfish and simply do whatever is best for us in any given situation?

The short answer, of course, is no. The reality we have all experienced is that selfishness and greed do not, in fact, make us happy. They may provide for some transient ecstasy but that is fleeting, and no real lingering happiness is left, and more often than not, quite the opposite. Lasting happiness does not occur for us on balance and more importantly, there is no elevation in the overall happiness of those around us (the victims of our greed). There is, in effect, a *net loss* in happiness when we are selfish due to the guilt and shame for the harm we've caused, and the unhappiness created in that very harm.

If we pursue transient states of ecstasy at the expense of more worthwhile and lasting satisfaction, we can find ourselves constantly seeking more and stimulation and in more novel forms. Materialism and greed are very much like drugs. Just as a junkie needs to have more and more of a drug in order to get the same fix, people who are addicted to 'things' need more and more of those things in order to try to achieve the satisfaction they are looking for. For example, how many people remain satisfied with the same car for any length of time? Be it a Ferrari, a Porsche or a Toyota, there comes a point very shortly after taking possession when it becomes 'just another car'.

- ❖ We strive for an objectively happy life.
- ❖ Our actions create this happiness and the virtue of our actions should ultimately be determined by how much happiness those actions create.
- ❖ The *journey* provides obstacles and challenges, and these are our chance to grow, learn, and evolve.
- ❖ We surmount the obstacles and challenges in life, in a way that leads to greater happiness, by having a moral compass that helps us to define our way.
- ❖ This moral compass is our **Credo.**

MY STORY

I have a strange jigsaw underpinning my moral basis. The first and biggest influence on me and my values is my Mum. For so many reasons, she is a towering figure in my life.

Mum was a devout Christian, and while she went to physical church less frequently as time went by, she always held her faith and this was the foundation of how she lived in the world. Interestingly, despite being so strong in her Christian faith, she was never conversional. She recognised that in a spiritual sense, 'all roads lead to Rome' and she never pushed the Christian faith on me or my sister. In fact, our parents decided that we would not be baptised into the Church because they felt that we would make the appropriate decision, for ourselves, when the time was right. Suffice to say, I never did get that baptism! Ma brought me my first books on Hindu philosophy and Buddhism, and they became the foundations of my spiritual life.

My Dad was and is agnostic, but he leads what I could only describe as a 'spiritual' life. He introduced me to Yoga and Eastern philosophy when I was a young child in the early 1980s. He initially became interested in Yoga as a way to become more flexible for marathon running but came to realise that these were practices that were so much more than stretching and entailed ways of acting to improve one's lot in this life, and also, were not dogma. To him, the concept of 'God' was simply not important to living a good life. He is a hedonist, in the sense of an ethical hedonist, not someone who is selfishly seeking pleasure, but someone for whom pleasure and experience are not just merely enjoyable, but the point of life, and are a spiritual journey in and of themselves. He is a master of stopping to smell the roses (or the wine!) and it is only with age that I have appreciated the spirituality within his truly experiential existence.

I initially rebelled against the Christian teachings, not those of my Mum really, but those that were forced upon me as a child at a Christian school. And my Mum supported me in that rebellion. She hit the roof when the Reverend at our school stated that "Children with the devil in them don't glow, and you Mr Harvey, do not glow!". She told that old wowser not to dare ever say anything like that to her son again. For that and the many other ways that she defended my spiritual freedom, I can't thank my Ma enough. She was the archetype of a 'true' Christian, who lived in Christ and was an example for others. She wasn't someone who expected you to do as they say but instead was an example of someone that you wanted to be like, because she lived her values.

After drifting through school, not really having to exert much effort to do well in class and particularly in exams (which came easily to me) and spending probably more time on flights of fancy, independent learning, and sports, I eventually found myself on borrowed time at high school. I struggled with severe depression through my teen years and I began to feel more and more stifled. A story for another time is that I was asked to leave school for wearing a skirt, but the coaches of the high school rugby 1st XV team of which I was the captain, intervened and allowed me to at least stay through to the end of the rugby season. What a contradiction! The nail-polish and skirt wearing jock of the school!

It was through my love of rugby that I became enamoured with the structure and function of the human body and this led me to study strength and fitness training, and nutrition at University. I felt I had finally found something which I was passionate about, that could also translate into a career. It would also give me a chance to show my Mum that I wasn't a fuck-up and that her trust in me was not misplaced. Being kicked out of nutrition class at Uni (but given a pass!) probably wasn't the best start to that but as I approached the end of the year and graduation, it was clear that I would at least have a qualification under my belt along with a brand-new business that I was starting with one of my buddies from Uni.

Things were underway!

But my Mum never got to see that business, nor any of the (albeit humble) successes that I have since achieved. She passed away the night before I was due to open my first nutrition supplement store and consultancy. I lived at home at the time, and when she collapsed in the middle of the night from an asthma-attack I tried, unsuccessfully, to revive her with CPR for what seemed like an eternity, continuing to help the EMTs when they showed up. I never really came to terms with her passing, and in retrospect, I think that was because I was so engaged with the process of trying to save her that I never really accepted, either in-the-moment or maybe even later (maybe even now?) that she was *actually* gone. I felt guilt and shame for not being able to save my Mum and that is a burden that has weighed heavily on me.

Mum's passing was the single biggest event in my life. I have been punched on the street, attacked with a bottle in a small town in Argentina, held up at gunpoint, threatened with a knife; I've won world titles and set world records, but nothing compares to losing my Mum, that night, at that critical time of my life and no weight that I have hoisted compares to carrying my Ma's coffin.

I hadn't had a particularly 'straight' life up to that point. I had done my fair share of drug-taking and drinking, from an altogether too young age. I began smoking pot and drinking heavily from about the age of 11 and took whatever drugs I could get my hands on from that age until I became involved in weight training and nutrition at around the age of 17. That gave me a few years of sobriety and a respite in which I developed habits of health and wellness that thankfully were able to re-emerge later.

But after Mum died, I was alone, metaphorically mostly, but somewhat in reality, too. My Dad was around but emotionally absent. I don't blame him, because he needed to find his way through his own turmoil at losing his soul mate. He did that with his mates and at times with the bottle. He never lashed out at us and was always there for us if we asked for help but for a while, he really just wasn't *around*. My sister too spent her time with her friends, and I with mine…and like father, like son, also with the bottle. But when I do things, I like to do them well, and so, unlike my Dad, I also added pills, speed, acid, mushrooms, and really anything else that could distract and dull the pain to the mix. The drugs also provided the energy to keep on moving. I was angry at the world and angry at people around me and I distracted myself with work, with drugs, and by covering up my pain with brash and bravado.

I still started that little business with my buddy from Uni and we were successful…really successful. But that success was due to our brains and our personalities and the ability to think on our feet (despite our brains being somewhat addled by intoxicants and lack of sleep!) We were the right guys, at the right time, doing the right things...but also doing plenty of the wrong things...

We succeeded despite what else we were doing. We would be out on a Monday, Tuesday, Wednesday, Thursday, Friday, and Saturday night. Sunday afternoons and evenings would usually be for sleeping...but not always. Despite that, I still went to work, 7 days a week from 8 am until 6 pm, not to mention the 1-hour minimum travel time each way, battling traffic to and from work, which was across the other side of the city from where I lived. This 'life' was not much of a life and after those first few years, I found myself burnt out and suffering from serious chronic fatigue. I became sick, lost most of the muscle I had gained over the previous years and struggled to even make it out of bed. That took away my ability to party (good ☺) and lift weights (not good ☹). It also forced a massive re-evaluation of who I was, what I was doing, and who was around me. I realised, through the haze of my fatigue and pain, that my business partner had become a drug addict, that many of the people around us were, quite frankly, losers, and that we were at serious risk of falling deeper into the underworld of crime and violence that we were skirting, of which, for my safety and sanity's sake, I will say no more!

But I needed out. So, I sold my share of the business to my partner. He went on to not pay me what I was owed, and he fell in with a well-known shyster who cajoled him into ripping off many innocent people in retail scams. Despite the large amount of money that I lost, looking back, it was the best decision to get out. Years later I reconciled with my business partner, who apologised for the way he treated me and at that singular moment, I let go of any resentment or anger towards him. We were stupid kids and we got tied up in stupid shit. I forgave him and came back to a place of love. Unfortunately, he remained embroiled in drugs and later, he committed suicide. I'm sorry that I couldn't have been around for him more but by that stage, I couldn't be around any of that junk for my own safety's sake.

The years following took many twists and turns. From working as a consultant to major food and supplement corporations, through to helping to run one of the top strength-and-conditioning companies in Canada. I have written seven books, worked with hundreds of top-level athletes, and many, many more people with severe and debilitating illnesses, and have been on a post-graduate journey that has included study in mind-body healthcare and masters and doctoral research in nutrition, specifically ketogenesis and 'Carb-Appropriate' diets. Through this time, I've also faced some health battles of my own. Starting at high school but worsening in my twenties and again reaching crisis several times through my 30s, I have fallen into deep, suicidal patterns of depression. It was only more recently that this was properly diagnosed as type 2 bipolar disorder. I have to step back and look at the benefits this has provided me. While the depression has been at times debilitating, the hypomania has expressed as boundless energy, inspiration, work ethic and creativity that has allowed me to do so many of the things for which I am proud, and I am the proudest overall of how the work created by this energy has helped other people. I also suffered physically with autoimmune conditions. I was diagnosed with Crohn's Disease at the age of 20 and while the worst effects of this; losing massive amounts of blood, suffering acute fatigue, anaemia, and losing around 20 kg of body weight, were relatively short-lived, some of the chronic effects that I suspect are tied into a complex of inflammation and auto-immunity (chronic pain and fatigue especially) and that are also linked to the mental health 'stuff', have been, shall we say, an ongoing project. Despite these health battles, I was able to come back from the worst effects of Crohn's Disease, recover my bodyweight and strength, and win two world titles in All-Round Weightlifting, also setting world records, and performing feats of strength on television and in exhibitions.

After giving away strength sports due to a severe back injury in which two of my spinal disks are basically, well, not even there anymore, I moved back into martial arts, Muay Thai, boxing, and eventually finding my 'forever home' in the world of grappling, catch-wrestling, and Brazilian Jiu-Jitsu. Interestingly, I was told years after becoming interested in grappling through Judo as a kid and reinterested via grappling and BJJ, that my grandfather had been a prodigious catch-wrestler who had bested the American champion in an exhibition match in New Zealand, and my Dad was also a Judoka when he was younger.

Some of those feats of strength, for those interested (at a bodyweight of under 75 Kg) were a one-handed deadlift of 180 Kg, A 'rack' deadlift of 385 Kg, and lifting an 'Inch Dumbbell' replica with one hand.

I had always, from my earliest years been a seeker. I don't say that in some smarmy, self-aggrandizing way. People use 'seeker' to pump themselves up. I don't mean that. I mean that I was, and still am, a seeker, because I know jack-shit!

I've wondered long and hard about why we are here. What's the goddamn point of it all and how the fuck do we live a healthy, happy life and help to spread that to others? And while I screw up with great regularity, over the years, my spiritual practice has evolved and more importantly, I have become comfortable in my own skin. At times I truly thought I had 'it'. I felt like 'enlightenment' was just around the corner. But seriously, fuck that! What the fuck is enlightenment anyway? I guess those who are truly wise are correct. If you think you have it, or you think you're close, you're probably as far away from it (whatever that is) as you can be.

Through the years, I found myself praying with Muslims at Sufi meetups, meditating with Buddhist monks, doing extensive transformational breathwork, conscious communication training, living in a meditation house in Vancouver, and continuing with a practice of mindfulness meditation and yoga. Somewhere along the way, I stopped thinking about how awesome and goddamn spiritual I was (look at me, look at me, *I'm special*) for doing these practices and instead just kept on in the process of **doing**, *come what may*.

Some of the comfort in my own skin and continuing to simply *do the work* while releasing some of the ego-attachment to it came from losing it all…

After taking a break from clinical practice due to burnout, I spent the best part of a year travelling in South America, taking the time to think and write (I wrote my first book 'Choosing You!' in the beautiful barrio of San Telmo, Buenos Aires, Argentina). Coming back to New Zealand, I was in a good space, mentally, physically, and emotionally, but shortly after arriving back, my partner didn't come home one night. I found out the following day that she had run off with her ex-boyfriend and was now living back with him. Boo-hoo, poor me. My problem after this was that I wanted to hold on to *everything*. We had some shared property and I wanted to hold on to it all because, well, fuck her, that's why. I was naïve and pig-headed and having had quite a lot of success at an early age, I didn't think I could put a foot wrong. Sometimes though, when you try to hold on to it all, you lose it all instead. The global financial crisis of 2007-2009 hit and my property values crashed, while at the same time the heat went out of the residential rental market. So, I was left for relatively long periods of time with greatly undervalued properties that were not returning any income. I held on to them by propping up the mortgage repayments with my life savings and by selling shares. I figured things would come right. It didn't help that I also decided to move to Canada to get away from it all and so, I wasn't around as much as I needed to be to really manage the properties and investments in the way that I should have in an economic situation like that! I realised my folly too late and in order to come out relatively unscathed, I had to sell both my properties when I could have probably been in-the-clear if I had sold just one, earlier.

Don't get me wrong, I had a great time in Vancouver, Canada, and stayed there for around four years. I met and worked with pro-athletes, partied with rock stars, and capped off my OE by helping to road-manage my best mate's band, *Like A Storm* (now NZ's most successful hard-rock band….ever!) for six months on tour around the US and Canada. But I also suffered from a huge ego-hit, especially when I finally returned to NZ. I hadn't realised how much my perception of my self-worth would be affected by losing everything. And by everything, I'm not being overly dramatic. I had sold my properties, having previously sold my shares and stripped my savings to support them, and had, over a few years been supporting myself with the aid of the kind people at the credit card companies. I had a shitload of credit card debt, nothing left in the bank and when I came home to NZ, I had an epiphany at Starbucks…

Having been in the US and Canada for a good while, Starbucks was pretty much the *lingua franca* for coffee. Come on, it's pretty good. It's consistent and offers fair-trade, organic options…but I digress. I went to my local Starbucks for a coffee and to do some writing like one of those jack-off wannabe poets who sits in a café writing their perpetually unpublished works to impress god knows who… I ordered my coffee and, lo and behold, my card declined. I left, checked my balance, and realised that the only card I had with any money left on it, had a balance of $2.37.

Fuck!

Now, when I say I lost everything, I am only talking about the material. I had the support of my sister (who let me stay with her rent-free for a while) and my Dad, an electrician, who gave me a short-term contract job painting a commercial building and working with him as an electrician's labourer to get enough money to start getting back on my feet. Plus, I'm a straight white dude and I'm fully aware of the implicit advantage that provides!

Long story short, I got back on my feet, started my clinic, was lucky enough to be involved with *Nuzest* as a co-founder/formulator and since then have started or reimagined several successful ventures, including *Nutrition Store Online, reconditioned.me* and *The Holistic Performance Institute*, along with writing another half dozen or so books.

Most importantly, and what I am most proud of, through my 22 years in practice, I've been able to help thousands of people to improve their health, their performance, and their happiness.

My main drive in the years ahead is to be able to help more people, especially those who can't always access good, evidence-based, holistic healthcare because of their social and economic position.

But wait! There's more...

Nutrition, exercise, sleep, and other facets of overall health are so very crucial...BUT I firmly believe they are the foundation, not the goal. They provide the physical, and neuropsychophysiological (mind-body) launching pad for the next step, which is to go beyond the material, beyond the physical, into deeper realms of experience and understanding that elude description within the frames of understanding that we have. Words and explanation can only allude to truths, they can never fully encapsulate the totality of metaphysical experiences. These realisations can be accessed through meditation and mindfulness, introspection, breathwork, and psychedelics.

The bridge between the foundations of health, and the ability to launch into deeper realms and to pursue a life of creativity, passion, and purpose, is to have a *Credo*, a set of guidelines that helps you to stay committed to your path of understanding. This credo allows you to do *the work* of being. It's not enough to *want* to be a better person or to *want* to live a better life, to achieve more, to know more, to feel more, and to help more. You must *do*.

It's not the spark that starts
the fire, it's the air you
breathe that fans the flames

Over the Rhine

A note on reflections

These are designed to help you be more introspective about the things that are not serving your highest purpose. Play with these ideas and concepts and spend some time in meditation or reflection just thinking about them and how you might change your life for the better.

A note on commitments

These are powerful, present tense, personal, and emotionally compelling statements of being that can help you to shift limiting subconscious beliefs and encourage powerful, new patterns of action. If these don't resonate with you, feel free to alter them to you and your life.

HONESTY

How often do you lie?

For many of us, it's a daily occurrence. We tell the 'little white lies' that make life easier, that help to expedite projects, and that 'let people down easy'.

We justify to ourselves why this is OK... But once we set ourselves on the path of little white untruths, they can all too easily become big hairy audacious lies.

Living an honest life isn't easy because there are so many subtle ways that we are encouraged to be less than truthful in the modern world. But honesty is the key to living a happy life and that's why it's the first tenet of *The Credo*. Seriously. It makes life easier. When you tell lies, you end up casting a bigger and bigger web of deceit which ends up being simply exhausting!

Beginning to live honestly and authentically is hard though. We think that we need to be 'perfect'. We think that we need to go back and tell everyone that we were ever less-than-honest with, that we lied to them. I don't think we need to do that, well not straight away at least. We all make mistakes and the key is to learn from those mistakes and not repeat them. I'm a big fan of doing what can be done, easily, and so, the easiest way to start to live with authenticity and honesty, is to start NOW. That means from this point on (right freakin' now…no excuses) anything that comes out of your mouth is the straight-up truth.

I remember working with a client in the mind-body area of my clinical practice. We were working on this tenet of living authentically and living *in* honesty. She was incredibly scared of being 100% honest with those around her because she had suffered tremendous trauma and abuse through her life and to, all of a sudden, have that be out in the open, even to those she loved, was far too painful. It was a good reminder that our safety is critically important as we move into honesty.

We worked together on making sure that from that moment onwards, anything that she put out into the world, from words through to actions, was honest and authentic. The rest of the 'stuff' from her past was left up to her. As she began to feel safer and more secure in herself and began to develop a true sense of empowered self-worth, she was able to open up to those people closest to her and talk about some of the untruths that she had used in the past to protect herself.

Remember that you are in control. If you feel unsafe, there is powerful action in *inaction*. You need not shout from the rooftops all of your past foibles and missteps...BUT from this moment on, you can live in truth.

HONESTY IS THE FIRST CHAPTER IN THE BOOK OF WISDOM

THOMAS JEFFERSON

Reflection:

Think back over your last 48 hours. How many little white lies (or big-ass lies!) did you tell? How did this make you feel? How could you put this right?

If you're able (and you feel safe doing so) go back and own up to your bullshit and tell the person/s that you have wronged, the truth.

Commitment:

From this moment on, I only speak the truth.

HUMILITY

In this modern age, we are expected to continually 'up' ourselves. We feel an enormous weight of expectation that we should be seen to be great – whatever the fuck that looks like...

We have the expectation from the stories and images that we are inundated with through media, that we need to be prettier, be leaner, be more muscular, be smarter, and be richer... But all these 'ers' require that we create a façade of being superior to others. Of course, we *can* create these facades, but all that leads to is all of us seeing only the collective façades that we and others project, not the reality of our own beautiful yet flawed existences.

These façades of perfection pervade social media; the perfect holiday, the perfect smoothie, the perfect ass...

This environment of media can make us feel like crap! Our baseline self-image can become one of feeling perpetually unworthy (of love, of respect, of appreciation, or of happiness) because we have created an inherent expectation of a completely unrealistic and unrealisable 'perfection'. We might then begin to seek to feel better by continuing to try, and try again, ad infinitum, to create our own façades of perfection.

But it's bullshit.

There is always someone better at something than you and always someone worse.

'What' you are is completely unimportant. You're not some special little flower that should be respected and appreciated as of right. You gotta earn that shit! What you *do* is the only metric for how you should be perceived. Now, I'm not suggesting that there shouldn't be baseline respect for all – of course, there should be. We should (and can) love everyone, as all human beings are worthy of being on this planet and have the basic rights and considerations that we would expect for ourselves.

BUT, once we begin to feel *entitled* to anything when we feel outraged that we're not loved enough, or respected enough, or appreciated enough, we're simply wasting our time. That's when you need to drop that shit and actually *do something*!

Do something that fills with you with passion and purpose. Do something that helps others and helps the planet.

Find a passion, do it well, forget about whether or not you'll become famous, or loved by others. DO IT FOR YOURSELF. So, be humble. Forget about the outcomes of fame and notoriety and forget about what people will think of you. Stop craving others love and respect and trying to gather it! Simply DO the right thing. BE a good person. LIVE to your values and the results will present themselves.

IT IS NOT THE MOUNTAIN WE
CONQUER BUT OURSELVES.
YOU DON'T HAVE TO BE A
FANTASTIC HERO TO DO
CERTAIN THINGS. YOU CAN
BE JUST AN ORDINARY CHAP,
SUFFICIENTLY MOTIVATED TO
REACH CHALLENGING
GOALS. PEOPLE DO NOT
DECIDE TO BECOME
EXTRAORDINARY. THEY
DECIDE TO ACCOMPLISH
EXTRAORDINARY THINGS

SIR EDMUND HILARY

Reflections:

How often do you compare yourself to others?

Are you addicted to either comparing yourself to others on social media or to constantly seeking approval and endorsement online?

Sidebar: You might want to try going on a social media 'diet'. Remove the apps from your phone and only use the web versions. Limit the time you spend on social media to 1-2 'blocks' per day and use a plug-in like 'Newsfeed Eradicator' for Facebook.

Commitment:

I am who I am, no more, no less.

I recognise my strengths and weaknesses and I strive to be the best I can be.

RESPECT

When we're honest and humble, a natural consequence is that we begin to have more respect for others. We can become so tied up in our own BS ideas of ourselves, that we forget that everyone struggles, and everyone succeeds, everyone has value, and everyone has done some bad shit too.

Respect doesn't mean that you have to like everyone, and it certainly doesn't mean you have to like what people do but it does mean that you need to give people the same level of fairness that you would demand of them. It's really the basis of the golden rule "do unto others as you would have them do unto you."

There is a fundamental baseline level of respect that we need to have for all people, irrespective of who they are what they have. That is human decency. Of course, that doesn't mean that we don't also temper our actions and who we decide to be around or take counsel from, based on the qualities that the person expresses. But we also need to be very careful of falling into the trap of absolutism.

For example, one might compare the biographical sketches of two people. One is an imperialist and classist, born into wealth, who was a drunk, a misogynist and avowed racist who supported the massacre of indigenous people in British colonies. The other, an animal-loving vegetarian teetotaller, who championed the rights of the ordinary working man.

Of course, smarty-pants people recognised the first person as Winston Churchill, championed as the greatest wartime leader of recent history, the other, Adolf Hitler, the leader of a regime that exterminated up to half of all Jewish and Romani people in Europe. While these biographical descriptions are intentionally incomplete, they also speak to the absolutism of 'good' vs 'bad' and 'good over evil'. Not one person is solely 'good', nor another 'bad'. We each exemplify the angel and the demon, and we are all complex and nuanced. On balance we might feel that someone is overwhelming more 'good' than 'bad' but if we are not very careful, we can begin to deify some people and vilify others as only good or bad, when in fact it is not so simple. That's why it's crucial to have some level of underlying respect for people and for the goodness in them, while also championing right-action and holding people accountable for the harms that they have committed.

Have respect and love for everyone. They all have their good points, even if they have many bad points. And have some respect for yourself while you're at it. While you're not 'better' or 'worse' than anyone else, you have value.

Straight up.

BE KIND, FOR EVERYONE YOU MEET IS FIGHTING A GREAT BATTLE

PHILO

Reflections:

How often do you exercise fundamental respect for others? Do you respect those you see sitting in traffic? Do you respect another's opinion and listen to them in a debate or discussion?

Do you congratulate your adversaries (in business, in sports, or any other field of human endeavour), or do you ignore them or make excuses for your loss, or crow about your victory?

Commitment:

I respect all people.

LOYALTY

My Dad always said *you dance with the one that you brought.* So, if you take a guy or gal to the dance, dance with him or her!

It's a quaint saying and seems a bit archaic but it still says so much about what we don't do enough of.

Loyalty is perhaps the biggest challenge and it might be harder, day-to-day, to practice being loyal than to live with authenticity and respect. On the other hand, if you get the other things right (honesty, humility, and respect) you might not need to focus so much on loyalty because it'll just happen.

The main obstacle to loyalty is the small moments of indecision. We often have committed to something but, late in the piece, something more exciting, or more tantalising comes up and we ditch our first option. I get it, sometimes we need to make a call because there is a greater opportunity available, AND if that choice is made with honesty and integrity, it's not to say it's a bad one. However, this is seldom the case. More often than not we let the opportunity for short-term and transient excitement overwhelm sticking to our word. Over the long-term, we will be far more respected and appreciated for being true to our word rather than for chasing flights of fancy.

How would you rather be known? As the person who waits until the last minute to see what better option might arise? Or as the person who is there, come hell or high water, to support their mates?

I can think right now of a handful of people who I know would support me and actually *be there for me* at any time and for any reason, and those people are my dearest, lifelong, and heartfelt friends.

DANCE WITH THE ONE YOU BROUGHT

MY DAD

Reflections:

Take a moment to think back on the times that you might have dipped out of a dear friend's event to pursue something you felt, at the moment, was more exciting. How did that work out? Do you feel good about it now?

Think back on other times in which you may have betrayed the confidence or wishes of someone dear to you. How has that changed your relationship with that person? Can you use those moments as a chance to grow? How can you *be* more loyal in future?

Commitment:

I am loyal.

COURAGE

Having values takes a lot of courage. I'm talking here about values that you actually LIVE, not the BS values that pundits claim to have yet don't live. A lot of people claim to have values, morals, and a strong ethical foundation...but they don't. They simply talk the talk, without doing any damn walking!

To have a credo that propels you to be better and to live and love better isn't easy. It requires the courage to take a stand and in doing so, to stand out. It requires actions like owning your bullshit, telling the truth (yes, telling the truth is a courageous act), and risking missing out on something if it will in any way hurt someone you love. It takes courage to do the right thing, even if it means you won't get to bask in the sunshine of fame or have a few extra dollars in your bank account.

But I'll tell ya something... It's simply better to live within the freedom of truth, humility, respect and love.

A big part of courage comes from knowing what you actually a) stand for, and b) what you really want out of life. What you stand for is, in a nutshell, your Credo, and this book provides, I hope, a starting point for that. What you really want out of life is the subtext to this. While your Credo is the BIG stuff that is important morally and ethically to your life and infuses through everything else, there is subtext to this and that is what your ethos and value-set can really define. These are the things that are congruent with your Credo, that you want and need to have in your life of passion and purpose in order to make it an objectively desirable life!

YOUR VALUES & ETHOS

Asking yourself WHY you work, why you play, in fact, why you do any goddamn thing is a great way to determine what is most important to you. In other words, it's a great way to figure out your values and ethos.

If for example, I asked myself why *I* have been in health and wellness practice for going on 22 years (at time of writing) I might answer, to serve others, or to create a positive impact on health and wellness in society, to help people to be healthier and happier, to continue to learn and grow, and to create financial security for me, my friends and my family.

Those of you who have read any of my other work or taken one of my courses will know that I always have my students start by asking why… and then asking why again and again until they have a clear and compelling reason or set of reasons why the *really* want to do something.

Here are some leading questions that can help you to finetune your ethos and value-set.

❖ *How do you fill your space? (E.g. At home, at work)*

❖ *How do you spend your spare time?*

❖ *How do you spend your work time?*

❖ *On what activities do you spend most of your energy?*

❖ *What do you spend most of your money on?*

❖ *Excluding rent and food, what do you spend the most money on?*

❖ *On what do you feel you spend most of your energy?*

❖ *In what area of your life do you feel you are most organised?*

❖ *What do you spend most of your time thinking about?*

❖ *What do you most dream about doing for a living?*

❖ *What do you most dream of doing as a hobby?*

❖ *What do you most dream about having?*

❖ *What do you talk about most?*

❖ *In what area of your life are you most passionate?*

❖ *In what area of your life do you set most of your goals?*

❖ *What inspires you most?*

❖ *Who inspires you most?*

❖ *Does my current life define or defy my values?*

How do your answers make you feel? Are your relationships to your environment, your work, and your play positive or negative? What do all these answers tell you about your ethos? How could you live more in line with your true inner values?

Now, determine the 3-5 most common themes. These can form your value-set and should be considered whenever a challenge or opportunity arises – does it *fit* with my values?

THE COURAGE TO CHANGE

Another aspect of courage is to have the strength to change your position. Our very identity, our personal *brand* can become tied up with a particular dogma especially if we have gained some notoriety, fame, or financial success through this. It can, therefore, be incredibly difficult to change position, even when we know that our former position is either partially or completely incorrect! That's one of the reasons I have so much respect for my colleagues at AUT University. Formerly highly critical of my stance on low-carbohydrate diets (if you're not aware of my work in nutrition—I'm a researcher in low-carbohydrate and ketogenic diets), they are now some of the leading researchers in this area. They could see that the evidence for the existing dietary guidelines (extremely high-carbohydrate, and low-fat) were not serving the public well, and so, they were prepared to change their stance at the risk of ostracization from the cohort of 'orthodox' nutrition and public health researchers and practitioners.

Which is not to say that I have always gotten it 'right' and that others have fallen into line with me because I'm so goddamned awesome. Far from it. I've had misfires, changes of heart, and most frequently, subtle shifts in my views on nutrition and health that have resulted from advances in the research, challenges from others, and healthy, robust debate. It's been difficult at times to be pragmatic and to, when necessary, kill our sacred cows, but it is imperative for our further growth and development and even more than that, it's imperative for living life with integrity. But it requires courage and strength.

Being courageous naturally involves having *brave conversations*. I was talking with my good friend Sarah many years ago about how we communicate and how all of us can learn to communicate more effectively and she framed this as 'having brave conversations'. I simply loved that terminology. It was so evocative and is the perfect terminology for those things that really need to be said, but seldom are.

THE SECRET TO HAPPINESS IS FREEDOM... AND THE SECRET TO FREEDOM IS COURAGE

THUCYDIDES

Reflections:

Is there something that you've been holding off on telling someone? Maybe it's telling your boss that you need a raise, or to move on. Maybe, it's owning up for something you royally fucked up?

What's holding you back? What is the fear? Where is the fear? Why are you afraid?

Now, suck it up buttercup. It's better to say what needs to be said, rather than leaving it to fester. You will thank yourself for doing it.

Commitment:

I am courageous.

PART 2. CREATIVITY, PASSION, AND PURPOSE

I could have left the book at the previous 5 virtues. They are a great foundation for living a life of integrity and will, no doubt, help to provide the 'razors' for your actions that will make life objectively far more desirable.

But, let's face it, they are a little dry and lack something…and that something is the joy of creativity, passion and purpose. Without creativity, we can become an automaton. Sure, we might be a 'good' person, but will we truly be happy?

Nope!

And what's more, without the leverage of passion and purpose, we can't fully explore our creativity and translate it into creations of value that benefit both our life and the lives around us.

MY MISSION IN LIFE IS NOT
MERELY TO SURVIVE, BUT TO
THRIVE; AND TO DO SO WITH
SOME PASSION, SOME
COMPASSION, SOME
HUMOUR, AND SOME STYLE

MAYA ANGELOU

CREATIVITY

Many people suffer from the mistaken belief that they aren't creative. But they're wrong… While they may not be innately creative in the artistic pursuits of music, painting, sculpture, poetry or prose, everyone IS creative and can develop that creativity.

There are two important points to be made here:

1. creativity is a skill, and like any other skill, it can be learned and improved.
2. many areas outside of what we traditionally can be termed 'creative pursuits can embody creativity, and this varies enormously between individuals.

In short, *you* are creative, you can become more creative, and you can exercise creativity in your chosen pursuits, whatsoever they may be. In fact, almost anyone who develops some higher level of skill in any arena is almost without exception, creative. Sure, there are journeymen and -

women who achieve success through a strong work ethic and by consummately developing their skillset but most people who succeed at the very highest levels do so as a result of not just skills and doing *the work* (both of which are essential) but also by bringing creativity to what they do. Think of sports. Most people think that sporting pursuits are purely physical but to watch any great sportsperson is to see an amalgam of work-ethic, consummate skills, AND creativity, passion, and purpose. No one watching Michael Jordon playing basketball, or Muhammed Ali box could make any sound argument that they are not witnessing a form of art.

I remember rolling (the Brazilian Jiu-Jitsu term for sparring) with Eddie Bravo, the first American to beat one of the Gracie family in BJJ competition, in Vancouver many years ago. His entire school of grappling is built on creativity and he is a prime example of someone for whom the creative pursuit can never be removed from the physical.

The challenge is *allowing* oneself to be creative. We are limited by bullshit ideas of self, often drummed into us by well-meaning (or not so well-meaning) teachers, parents, friends and others, who told us to 'stop dreaming', to 'stop doing that', or 'you're just not an 'artist''.

The biggest difficult obstacle to creativity is belief.

We develop so many self-limiting beliefs; If we are not musically gifted when young, we're not musical; if we can't beautifully blend our pastels in kindergarten, we're not 'artists', if we're awkward playing sports as we go through a growth spurt, we're not athletic. All of this is bullshit because true art is not dependent on the conventional norm. 'Art' is absolutely subjective and more often than not, the breakthroughs that further humanity are, in fact, those that defy the conventional thinking and that initially are thought of as 'wrong'. This is not to say that any old splash of paint on a canvas has merit (it might, but it might not) or any random assemblage of notes will constitute what most people think of as music. There does need to be some foundation of skill to build on. This is exemplified by the saying 'you must learn the rules before you break them'. Picasso, for example, is often seen as being a purely abstract artist and many have said on seeing his most famous works; "I could have done that!", but a) they didn't, and b) no, they couldn't.

Picasso (notwithstanding his many flaws) was a consummate and skilled orthodox painter and sculptor, who used his incredible innate *and* learned skills to then expand into creative areas hitherto unventured. He learned the rules, then broke them.

Now, many of you might be reading this and thinking "I ain't no Picasso..." But, here's the rub...you don't need to be!

You don't need to be a ground-breaking artist (in whatever field, even those not considered 'art') but you do need to be creative.

Why?

Because creativity is integral to satisfaction. It is impossible to fully enjoy life without creativity (and passion and purpose as we shall see.) To live without it is not to live.

I suffered for many years believing I was not 'a creative'. I wasn't particularly gifted at the visual arts (although I was much better than my teachers and my self-limiting beliefs gave me credit for), nor at music or other supposedly creative pursuits. But, over time I began to realise that creativity was actually my biggest driver of action. I love to create! In fact, aside from the things I do in clinical practice – nutrition and mind-body therapies – I am most well known as a prolific content creator. I write books, articles, make podcasts and videos and a range of other content. In my spare time, I design gardens and make bonsai, plus I like to think of interesting ways to choke people out in my sport... and that shit's creative!

The most creative aspect of all that? Figuring shit out! I love having a problem and figuring out a solution and then helping others with the benefit of what I've discovered. THAT is my creativity, and I wouldn't be without it.

I remember one day I had lunch with my godfather Devo[i] and the CEO at the time of a major Telco in New Zealand. The CEO looked at my phone and said, 'You're not with us then?', because my phone wasn't supported by their network. The thing is, I was on their network because I had figured out how to make it work... The CEO's response; "You clever bastard!"

---

[i] Unfortunately, David 'Devo' Walden passed away several years ago, and I miss him each and every day.

CREATIVITY INVOLVES BREAKING OUT OF ESTABLISHED PATTERNS IN ORDER TO LOOK AT THINGS IN A DIFFERENT WAY

EDWARD DE BONO

Reflections:

What do you LOVE to do?

WHY do you love to do it?

What aspects of your job, your sport, or other areas are you creative in?

How could you become more creative in the areas of your life that you love?

Commitment:

I live in creativity

PURPOSE

Creativity is essential but creativity without purpose can't by its very nature lead to outcomes that improve our lives.

There is a place for the pure 'play' of creativity without needing an objective outcome. On the other hand, there are many things for which we will want to exercise our creativity towards an outcome, and that requires *purpose*. This could be, for example, writing a novel or a non-fiction book. A venture of that nature requires a commitment to a goal or in other words, purpose. Without it, you will never have the critical mass of words on paper that is a complete book. You may end up with a few chapters, or some prose that's interesting but not a book. There are millions of uncompleted books in drawers and dressers around the world that never *became* because the author lacked a clear vision and sense of purpose.

Purpose itself is the sum of having a clear intention or goal, along with the structure and process to achieve that goal, and most importantly, the resolve to continue to do *the work* to complete the project.

It is easy to start projects. When we are filled with inspiration, ('piss and vinegar' so to speak) we can begin something and make huge inroads. Inevitably though, there will come a point in time in which that initial rush of energy and inspiration wanes. It is then that our sense of purpose must be strong enough to translate into the resolve of continuing to work the process until we have completed the project.

How many books lie incomplete? How many PhDs are left 'ABD'? (Google it 😌)

Far too many, and mostly due to a lack of purpose.

Many might think that resolve is something that people are born with. And there do seem to be those for whom resolve, and purpose come easily. But most often resolve is a learned skill. We create our purpose by in turn creating the powers of habit that allow us to stay in-process and keep moving forward, no matter what challenges arise in the path to meet us. The more that we accomplish, despite these challenges, the stronger we become, and the stronger our sense of purpose becomes as a result.

YOUR PURPOSE IN LIFE IS TO FIND YOUR PURPOSE AND GIVE YOUR WHOLE HEART AND SOUL TO IT

SIDDHARTHA GAUTAMA

Reflections:

Have you started a grand project only to leave it idle once your energy waned? Is that project redeemable?

What BIG audacious goals do you have that you haven't started? Are you ready (hint: yes, you are...) to start that project now, set a goal and a process, and stick with it to the end?

Commitment:

I live my life with purpose.

PASSION

The final ingredient in the Credo is to live with passion. In many respects' 'passion' is the marriage of creativity and purpose. But it evokes more than that too. Passion is born of love and inspiration and it provides the ongoing energy to continue to pursue the things we love.

The question might arise; how can I become passionate?

Well, perhaps you can't...

Passion comes from finding the things that are important to living your desirable life (your ethos and value-set) and recognising the creative pursuits that allow that to be a reality. Remember that these need not be traditional artistic pursuits but can be in your job, your sport, or your hobbies.

The framework for living a life of passion (and purpose) is to follow the steps outlined earlier:

1. Figure out what your personal 'value-set' is.

What are the things that drive you and that you want to have in your life in order to make it the life you want to be living?

2. Figure out what drives your creativity.

   What are the pursuits that allow you to exercise your freedom? What aspects of your job, your sport, your art, or any other aspect of your life make your heart and soul sing?!

3. Integrate.

   How can you do more of the things you love and that embody your creativity? Do these a) align with your deepest ethos and values, and b) allow you to achieve financial freedom?

EVERY GREAT DREAM BEGINS
WITH A DREAMER. ALWAYS
REMEMBER, YOU HAVE
WITHIN YOU THE STRENGTH,
THE PATIENCE, AND THE
PASSION TO REACH FOR THE
STARS TO CHANGE THE
WORLD

HARRIET TUBMAN

One final note...

It is imperative to find a vocation or career that can embody your life of passion and purpose. What you do for the vast majority of your life MUST be congruent with your values and it must allow some degree of creativity that helps to drive your unique passion and purpose. This doesn't mean that you need to find the 'perfect job' because that, all too often is a fantasy. It becomes an 'ever retreating mirage' that people try to find and yet never can. More often, there are many (many!) jobs that are congruent with your ethos and that can drive both passion and purpose. The key is to reflect back on those BIG things that you have identified as integral to your ethos and then to consider all the many ways that you could express those values and all the many careers and vocations in which you could do that. You'll be surprised at just how many there are, and many people are often able to find exactly what they need in their current job or industry because what they needed was not a change of job, but a change of perspective.

However, if your job sucks ass. Ditch it. You're an adult and you make the rules for you.

PART 3.
INTEGRATION

I was ready to publish this book but didn't. I let it drag for a few months. I thought that I was just too busy to prioritise it and to give it the marketing push I felt it deserved. I figured there would be time...soon to do that. What I now realise in retrospect is that there was something missing, something lacking.

As I mentioned earlier in the book, there is a great metaphor for life and for the process of change in the words *it's not the spark that starts the fire, it's the air you breathe that fans the flames.* To me, the 'spark' is the shift that can happen, even instantaneously, in our self-belief from flashes of inspiration we have. However, these moments of inspiration are not enough to foster lasting changes and to create an objectively desirable life. It is the *air we breathe*, in other words 'the work', that allows us to take the epiphanies we have and translate them into patterns of action that help us to achieve extraordinary things. And the more we breathe, i.e. the harder we work, the more likely we will achieve that life we desire and deserve.

Here's the thing, if you don't believe that you can achieve greatness, you won't. On the other hand, if you believe you can, but don't do *the work* to get there, you will be equally disappointed.

In this section, you will learn critical, time-effective daily, weekly, and less frequent actions to integrate the Credo into your life.

I AM A GREAT BELIEVER IN LUCK.
THE HARDER I WORK, THE MORE OF IT I SEEM TO HAVE

COLEMAN COX

MINDFULNESS

A simplified definition of mindfulness is *the state of being aware.* This can be a little confusing for the mindfulness novice because while of course, you are 'aware' in the sense of being conscious, awake, and lucid, the meaning of awareness (or 'conscious') in relation to mindfulness is subtly, yet crucially different. While we are conscious (awake with normal brain function) and aware (able to respond/react to stimuli) in the standard sense, we are also reacting to the things that happen to us unconsciously, based on the conditioning created by a lifetime (or more) of experiences.

In other words, we are not *consciously* in control of much of what we do! Our actions are determined sub-consciously based on what is deemed to be most important for survival. While this is important to allow us to react in certain ways to external stimuli to keep us safe, our reactions are not always in keeping with our highest purpose.

Many of our reactions are built upon the traumas of youth, negative life experiences, and negative perceptions of self, Thus, we end up living out our day-to-day actions biased by our past and by the way our journey to this point has affected our self-belief and perceptions of self-worth.

Mindfulness helps us to cut through the bullshit stories we tell ourselves and see our human condition for what it is. It helps us to notice moment-by-moment that all things (including human thoughts and emotions) arise and fall away. We begin to not just learn but to truly and deeply become aware of the age-old wisdom that *this too shall pass*. Most importantly for the process of changing your life, mindfulness provides what I like to call a critical 'junction' of time in which you can become acutely aware of when you are about to react, playing out the same old negative shit, instead of responding in a way that is in line with your ethos. This becomes a crucial step in stopping those negative behaviours and turning them into positive, life-affirming habits that will help you to achieve your goals and perhaps, more importantly, learn to cherish the present moment.

It can seem self-indulgent and even a little silly to meditate in order to cultivate mindfulness and to some degree it is self-indulgent. But hey, what's wrong with taking just a few minutes each day for yourself? Like they say on the aeroplane, put on your own oxygen mask before helping others!

While it can also seem a bit weird and esoteric, the benefits of meditation to health and happiness have been so conclusively proven by scientific research that we would be remiss to not use this powerful tool.

The difficulty most people have, like most other things in life, is actually getting started. We resist any additional time taken from our day to do something new because we feel so time-pressured nowadays, even when there is likely to be a huge benefit. And most people do realise that there is a benefit. When I ask clients if they meditate, the most common answer I get is "No...but I know I *should*". Firstly, 'should' is bullshit. Either do or don't, there ain't no 'should' around here...

People do recognise that meditation is valuable, they just struggle to apply it and to create the habit of *doing it* each and every day. Many people don't feel that they have enough time, and yet find themselves procrastinating, watching YouTube vids, and scrolling the news for far longer than the time it would take to just DO a meditation. To break this time barrier, I typically ask my clients if they have just one minute to devote to meditation tomorrow.

One minute? *One minute?!* They say...

Yes, just one minute.

When we start with one minute and build minute-by-minute over consecutive days, we are training our 'meditation muscle' just as we'd train our biceps by increasing the repetitions and load that we use over time.

THE PRESENT MOMENT IS
FILLED WITH JOY AND
HAPPINESS. IF YOU ARE
ATTENTIVE, YOU WILL SEE IT

THICH NHAT HANH

Action:

Begin with one minute of mindfulness of breath, then increase your meditation by one minute each day until you reach ten minutes. Aim for at least 30 unbroken days of meditation.

Begin, over time, to incorporate awareness into other daily activities like walking, gym-work, art, and even mundane chores like washing the dishes or doing the vacuuming. You will find, at the very least, that the mundane becomes bearable and the desirable becomes magical!

Mindfulness of breath

❖ Find a quiet, comfortable place to sit

❖ Sit with your back straight and upright, with good posture, yet relaxed.

You may like to use a traditional posture such as a lotus or half-lotus position or sit on your heels with your knees folded under you. These postures were developed for meditation and are very effective. You can also sit in a comfortable chair with your heels flat on the floor and your back upright, supported by the back of the chair.

❖ Place your hands together comfortably in your lap.

❖ Close your eyes – but not tightly.

❖ Begin breathing in and out through your nose. Do not 'try' to breathe deeply or in any fashion; simply breathe comfortably and without effort.

❖ Begin to notice the sensation of the air passing in and out of your nose. There will be a point or area in your nostrils or on the outside rim where you will feel the breath as it moves in and out. Gently bring your attention to this area.

You may find that it helps to count the breaths initially. Count each in and out breath as one breath and count your breaths up to 10 if you find that this helps you get into the meditation.

❖ Keep 'watching' the breath; when your mind wanders, simply bring it back gently to the point where you can feel the breath. It's that simple…

I use the Mindfulness app *to time my meditations.*

iTunes: https://itunes.apple.com/nz/app/the-mindfulness-app-meditate/id417071430?mt=8

Android:
https://play.google.com/store/apps/details?id=se.lichtenstein.mind.en&hl=en

❖ Start with a one-minute meditation first-thing tomorrow morning.

❖ Add one minute each day until you reach 10 minutes.

❖ Meditate each day for 30 days straight.

❖ Don't break the chain!

GRATITUDE

Being grateful is a time-honoured way to learn to live in the moment and to begin to experience joy IN the moment. After all, it's hard to be down (or at least, as down as you were) when you have focussed on the many things that you can and should be grateful for in your life. Suffering and hardship are relative. Now, hear me out here... I don't mean to downplay anyone's life experiences or the traumas that they may have experienced but the old adage that there is always someone better off and someone worse off than us rings true. We all have many things that have hurt us in our journey to this point in our lives. Equally, we all have many (many) things that have given us joy and have brought us closer to those around us and those are the moments that we can give thanks for.

By being grateful, we attach to all that is positive in our lives. This helps to create a focus on positivity rather than that state into which we often fall, of focussing on the negative. When we focus on the positive, we are more likely to view obstacles as part of the journey and as challenges that can be overcome (it might even be fun!) as compared to threats which serve to 'stress us out'.

GRATITUDE TURNS WHAT WE HAVE INTO ENOUGH

ANONYMOUS

Action:

After your mindfulness meditation, think of 3 things in your life that you are really grateful for. Each day think of different and more and more meaningful things.

Over your day, try to bring this gratitude into your activities. Say thank you (and really mean it).

GRATITUDE AND FORGIVENESS

All things that have happened to us have made us the person we are today. When you're in a process of moving towards great achievements (for you, whatever they are) and are happy and comfortable with your life, all things that have made you, are, at least in some way, positive!

So, even those people who have hurt us, have taught us something. While it can be difficult to acknowledge those who have wronged and hurt us, as our teachers, the *experiences* have, in fact, taught us so much. We can give gratitude for both the learnings that have arisen from our trauma and also that we were able to come through it (high five kid…you're a survivor!)

In our gratitude practice, we can begin to acknowledge and give thanks for the hard times, as well as the good, and by doing this, to release our guilt, shame, and our anger towards others, and this can be the first step in forgiveness…

Forgiveness is, I think, a misunderstood topic. It does not mean that we release someone from culpability for their actions. It doesn't mean that we 'accept' their actions as being OK. It certainly doesn't mean that we would allow that same thing to happen to us again, or anyone else, if we can at all avoid it.

But it is important to forgive.

By forgiving, we are allowing ourselves to release the attachment to the trauma and to the guilt, shame, and anger that accompanies it. It is an acknowledgement that we have come out of the other side, that we have survived, stronger and more resilient than before, and that the person or people who have hurt us are no longer able to.

Unfortunately, in this life, people are hurt by others, and in the cruellest of ways. This can change them and push them towards cruelty and thus, the cycle of damage continues. We often dismiss just how close we all can be to becoming someone who is cruel and hurtful. When we demonise the actions of those who commit the most heinous of crimes, we seek to separate them from the rest of humanity. By doing so we reject our responsibility as part of humanity. We see them as monsters, as 'different', when in fact, ordinary people, conditioned to be so, can easily become what we call 'monsters'. Look at relatively recent experiences of people in Nazi Germany, Stalinist Russia, Mao's China, and Pol Pot's

Cambodia. While there were certainly psychopaths and sadists that were beyond the pale, there were also many, many normal people, coerced to do the most abnormal of things.

BE KIND, FOR EVERYONE YOU MEET IS FIGHTING A GREAT BATTLE

PHILO

For these reasons, as your gratitude practice deepens you might want to consciously begin to give thanks to the teachers you have had in life, and the lessons learned, even if those things were traumatic and hurtful. BUT remember to do this gently and slowly and if you feel at-risk in any way at all, contact a licensed mental health practitioner.

- ❖ After your meditation practice perform a gratitude exercise.
- ❖ Give deep and heartfelt thanks for three things in your life that are awesome!
- ❖ Over time, think of different, more meaningful (and more difficult) things t be grateful for in your life.

BELIEFS

Our beliefs are created over the entirety of our lives and are the basis for the semi-autonomic reactions discussed in the chapter on Mindfulness. Often, my patients are surprised to realise that they are constantly creating their set of underlying beliefs and *who they are*, moment-by-moment as they respond and react to the world around them. This epiphany shifts their thinking from one of 'I am who I am' to 'I create who I am'.

This is an extraordinarily powerful realisation to come to. Our self-limiting beliefs hold us back. Self-sabotage, procrastination and the other ways that we derail our progress are the results of these patterns of self-belief that we have co-created within our environment over the course of our lives. Henry Ford said, "Whether you think you can, or think you can't, you're right", yet this is not entirely accurate. You can *think* you can and yet subconsciously *believe* that you can't. If you *believe* that you can't, you most certainly will not!

Once we realise that we are not simply 'who we are' and that we can change the way we are, the way we act, and the results we can achieve, we are empowered to take a more active approach to life.

BELIEF + DOING 'THE WORK' =
RESULTS

ME

Action:

Identify and shift your self-limiting beliefs. This is not as difficult as it might at first seem. Simply notice the negative self-limiting things you say to and about yourself and the negative ways that you see and perceive yourself in your mind's eye. It can help to write these down so that you can work to 'flip' these negative beliefs into positive.

Once you have an idea of some of your big negative beliefs, you can start to shift these into positive belief patterns.

'Flipping' negative belief patterns

❖ Take one of the negative patterns that you have noted down.

❖ Think of the direct opposite to this and write that down.

❖ Now, look at what you have written down and ask yourself: Is it positive? Is it personal (first-person)? Is it powerful? Is it present tense?

❖ Change the wording of your new positive belief statement so that it is powerful, present-tense, personal, and positive. Make sure that it is emotionally compelling to you.

❖ Repeat this positive belief statement to yourself at least 3 times.

❖ A good time to do this exercise is after your gratitude and mindfulness, or any time that you feel you are becoming too negative.

Example:

I might be having a hard time with my state of self-worth around finances. I have found myself suffering from this in the past and it expressed as internal monologue of "I could NEVER afford that", "I'm not a success" and other similar thoughts.

I could 'flip' these with statements like "I am successful", "I attract wealth in abundance" or even "I am worthy of success". Note that all of these are personal (I), present tense (i.e. am) and positive.

❖ Notice your negative self-talk and imagery.
❖ Write it down.
❖ Change the framing of your negative beliefs to positive.
❖ Repeat these to yourself as positive, empowering personal mantras.

CHECK-INS

The end of the working day provides an opportunity to put a 'bookmark' in the day, close off our work mindset and focus on spending time with family, doing the non-work things we love and relaxing and unwinding. Many people find this very difficult to do though. Work commitments and projects can dominate our thoughts late into the evening, affecting our relationships, our attention to other things like non-work passions and hobbies, and reducing the length and quality of our sleep (which is critical to health.)

A 'ritual' to signal the end of the workday helps the mind and body to unwind and relax. This could be anything from a short meditation, a walk, through to doing some other type of exercise. It could also involve a 'check-in' to see how the day went, and more importantly, how it could have been improved.

In this check-in the idea is to, without any judgement, look back over the day that was and objectively recognise a) the things you did well and b) the areas that still need improvement. These are sometimes the same thing too!

By recognising when we have succeeded and done well, we allow ourselves the opportunity to enjoy our accomplishments, something that few of us take the time to do. By recognising those things that perhaps we did not do so well, or that were not in line with our values and ethos, we can make a mental note to act differently in future. With a firm intention on this, and by visualising powerfully how we would act in a similar future situation, we begin to train ourselves into habits of behaviour that are congruent with our ethos and values and that help us to achieve our goals, where previously our reactions may have derailed our progress.

This check-in is also a great opportunity to make a task list for the following day. My students and those who have read my books *Time Rich, Cash Optional* and *Time Rich Practice*, will know that I am a firm believer in having a short, daily 'to-do' list of no more than three critical items. I call this my 'Mission Critical' list. Every evening, at the end of my workday, I go over, in my mind's eye, how the day went and whether there were any areas I could improve. This only takes a few minutes. Then, I look at my general task list (which, like yours I'm sure, is very long!) and I pick out three critical tasks to do the following day. I cannot stress how important this is. Most of us have to-do lists...and for most of us, they are packed with a myriad of things that either need to be done or that we want to do and with varying degrees of urgency. But simply having a to-do list and looking at it in the morning or through the day is a sure-fire way to lose your effectiveness. When you look at the task list it can seem overwhelming and then, one of two things happens, 1) you do the easy tasks or the things that will take little time, not because you're lazy but because you want to *get shit done* and see the list shortening, or 2) you do only the 'urgent' things and forget about the important.

Not all urgent tasks are important and not all important tasks are urgent. There will be compliance tasks (like taxes) that are critical to do in a timely fashion (even though we'd rather not) and conversely, there are important tasks to *you* that aren't urgent at all.

For example, take writing a book. I have written eight books including this one, and co-authored others, and so, I'm often asked how to write books as it's a common desire to put one's thoughts and ideas down on paper...

My response is a simple one: write.

The problem with achieving a big, audacious goal like writing a book, is seldom having the desire to do it or even having ideas and inspiration. The first challenge is to start, and the even greater challenge is to keep going! One of the best pieces of advice I ever received was from my good friend and mentor Dr Ian Brooks. Ian is a highly successful author and speaker. When I approached him with my idea to write my first book, he told me "Cliff, finish your draft". This simple, yet powerful statement speaks to the inherent truism of completing any major goal. You have to start (in this case, your draft) and you need to be consistent, in this case, to have the critical mass of words on the pages.

That's why at least one of your **three** daily tasks should be something that is integral to working towards a longer-term goal that is important to you and your life of passion and purpose. The other two tasks can be urgent tasks that simply need to be done but, I reiterate that at least one should be something that is a daily, recurring task, that is putting you closer, step-by-step to one of your dream-goals.

Side-benefits of setting just three critical tasks are that you will be far more effective at prioritising the tasks that need to be done in the timeliest fashion while also working consistently towards goals, without being derailed by task confusion. You'll also begin to know the sense of freedom that comes from actually completing your (daily) task list! Once you have finished those three tasks, you know that you have done all that you *need* to do on that day and can then choose whether you do a little more 'work' (and feel like you're one step ahead) or take that extra time to play, create, or relax, in the surety that you are still on track to meeting your goals.

FINISH YOUR DRAFT...

DR IAN BROOKS

Action:

At the completion of each workday, look back over the day that was. See where you have lived in-line with your ethos and where you have lived counter to it. Resolve to change your future actions.

❖ Take a few minutes at the end of the workday to put the day's work aside and relax and unwind.

❖ Think back over the day and notice all the moments in which you lived according to how you want, vs when you acted out of line with your ethos and values.

❖ Resolve to change those times and think about what that might involve and how that might look and feel in the future.

❖ Set three critical tasks to do tomorrow.

❖ Make sure one of these is an important (not just urgent) task.

BREAKS

Taking breaks is essential to remaining healthy, mentally well, and on-track towards your life goals. Taking breaks can be on the micro (daily) or macro (weekly, monthly, or yearly) scale. It has been well demonstrated that taking breaks throughout your day can help you to be more effective and being more effective will help you to be happier. Put simply, if you're better at getting shit done (assuming it needs to be done!) you'll feel more satisfied and you'll have more time to focus on other things that don't 'need' to be done but that you want to do.

DAILY BREAKS

The Pomodoro method pioneered by Francesco Cirillo is perhaps the most well-known micro break strategy. It involves working for 25 minutes, then taking a 5-minute break, and after four work 'blocks' taking a 15-30 minute rest.

The idea behind doing relatively short blocks of work is two-fold. It helps to encourage increased focus on the task because after some time we may find our mind wandering off-task and thus, we become less productive and it also serves to refocus us consistently and in doing so, we can recognise in the moment when we are pursuing a topic or task that is actually not congruent with where we want to end up.

Later research has suggested a range of times up to an hour for the work block with varying break times of between 5 and ~15 minutes break. I typically work for around one hour, either relying on my Fitbit watch and the hourly movement reminder or by setting an hour for music to play on the brain-focussing music app *Brain.FM*. I'll then take a 5-10 minute break to get up, get a drink, do some stretching, or light exercises like callisthenics (handstand push-ups, pistol squats, pullups etc) or light club-bell or sledgehammer swinging.

SELF-APPOINTMENTS & WEEKLY BREAKS

Weekly breaks are also critical to your life of passion and purpose. I have often discussed with clients a strange anomaly we have... That is, that we set appointments, and keep them, with others. Like going to the doctor, or meeting with clients, and yet, we either don't set the same appointments for or with ourselves or when we do set them, we fail to keep those appointments. As a nutritionist and strength coach of over two decades experience, I have seen this many times. People set appointments with themselves to go to the gym, prepare food for the following day, or to meditate in the morning and yet, whenever anything else comes up (typically to serve someone else) they sacrifice their self-appointment for the other person.

This has to stop!

You MUST make and keep weekly appointments with yourself for those things that are important for your health and happiness. These should be scheduled into your diary just like any other appointment and kept with the same diligence. You cannot be of service to others if you're not being of service to yourself.

I'm also a big fan of a weekly break, similar to the old Judaeo-Christian 'sabbath'. Now, bear with me here. I'm not religious and I'm not Christian. But I do see huge value in some of the devices that have been created over millennia by many of the religious traditions. When we strip away the dogma, we can see that there is tremendous value in practices like meditation, prayer and surrendering to what will be, and giving thanks (i.e. gratitude).

Similarly, there is also value in an idea like the Sabbath, or a day of rest. In this modern world of ours, I take this to be a day in which you disconnect from online social media, spend time with family and/or friends, and spend time reconnecting to the people and the world around you, without the distraction of the facade that so often is the microcosm of social media. While I'm not always perfect with this, as a rule, I don't check social media at all on a Sunday and I try to spend that day with my partner, our dog, and my little bonsai trees. If I fail to do this, I notice a palpable increase in my stress levels the following week.

PERIODIC BREAKS

Periodically, it can be a good idea to check in and ask yourself with brutal honesty whether any of your habits have become a vice or crutch.

Do you rely on alcohol to unwind at the end of the day? Are you starting to smoke a bit too much pot? Are you eating lots of sugar to help to fill a void?

If you have become reliant on something, it's a great opportunity to take a break from it, for several days, weeks, or months to release the attachment.

Over longer timeframes, breaks are essential to staying fresh but more importantly, they are part of the goal anyway! Breaks in which you get away, learn and do interesting things are part-and-parcel of the values and ethos that you hold dear.

It's imperative to schedule these breaks in advance and make sure that they are a regular fixture in every year.

REST IS NOT IDLENESS, AND TO
LIE SOMETIMES ON THE GRASS
UNDER TREES ON A SUMMER'S
DAY, LISTENING TO THE
MURMUR OF THE WATER, OR
WATCHING THE CLOUDS
FLOAT ACROSS THE SKY, IS BY
NO MEANS A WASTE OF TIME

JOHN LUBBOCK

Action:

Take breaks throughout the day. Try using the 'Pomodoro' method, or a similar routine of work-break. Experiment with taking breaks from vices, habits, and most especially social media.

- ❖ Take breaks throughout your workday. Use these as opportunities to refocus, be mindful, and to breathe, stretch, and move.
- ❖ Try taking occasional breaks from vices or habits. For example, take a week or two, or a month off alcohol, or sugar, or another comfort-habit and reflect on how you feel. What did you learn from this process?
- ❖ Disconnect from social media on one day of the week and take the opportunity to connect directly and in-person with your partner, your family, your friends, and nature.

AFTER

This book was equally challenging and easy to write. It was challenging because I opened up for the first time about some of the difficulties I have faced, from losing my Mum and others, through battling drug and alcohol abuse, and the risk of falling into a life of crime. On the other hand, it was easy to 'flow' into the writing and expound these ideas that I see as so very important for living a happy and healthy life – ideas that have been sitting in draft form on my computer for many years.

Perhaps it wasn't the right time before. If I had published this book earlier, I think I would have been altogether too sanctimonious and too sure of myself. I would have really cared what people thought of me and how I would be perceived. I would have really wanted to be liked, respected and appreciated.

But now, after many more knocks and setbacks, I can't help but feel that I am in a better, more beautifully flawed place in which to write.

Overall though, I simply hope that it brings some inspiration to someone, somewhere in the world, and if that person is you, please reach out and let me know how it has inspired you.

WITH ALL IT'S SHAM, DRUDGERY AND BROKEN DREAMS, IT IS STILL A BEAUTIFUL WORLD... STRIVE TO BE HAPPY

MAX EHRMANN
(FROM THE *DESIDERATA*)

ABOUT CLIFF

Cliff Harvey is a researcher, registered clinical nutritionist, mind-body therapist, and former world champion and world-record holding strength athlete.

He has been coaching people ranging from world champion athletes through to the chronically and acutely unwell, and businesspeople and entrepreneurs, to perform at their best, since the 1990s.

Cliff's early post-graduate studies were in mind-body healthcare. His Master's research focussed on the use of medium chain triglycerides to mitigate 'keto-flu' and encourage faster induction of nutritional ketosis, and his Doctoral research on identifying markers of carbohydrate tolerance and appropriateness of different diets to individuals.

He is the founder of the Holistic Performance Institute, a private graduate college, and is the author of seven books including *The Carbohydrate Appropriate Diet, Time Rich Practice,* and the Ashton-Wylie Book Award finalist *Time Rich, Cash Optional.*

❖ www.cliffharvey.com

❖ twitter.com/carbappropriate

❖ facebook.com/cliffharveyauthor